BEHIND

SANTA'S SMILE

Behind Santa's Smile

Twenty Years as Santa Al

by Al Capehart

Book and Cover Design by Jane Dunlap
Jacket Photography: Front: The Picture People,
www.picturepeople.com / Back: Jane Dunlap
/ Photoshop edits by Kim Mikiel
Line Art in Text (SANTA AL logo) by Ethan Wenburg
Poster Art by Charles Dennis Wolfe / Photoshop edits by Chatham
Business Services, Pittsboro, NC

ISBN-10: 1492722529
ISBN-13: 978-1492722526

Publisher's Cataloging-in-Publication data
Capehart, Albert Cowardin.
    Behind Santa's smile : twenty years as Santa Al / Al Capehart.
    p. cm.
    ISBN 978-1492722526
1. Capehart, Albert Cowardin. 2. Santa Claus. 3. Christmas --Anecdotes. 4. Christian life. 5. Spiritual memoir. 6. North Carolina
--Biography. I. Behind Santa's smile : 20 years as Santa Al. II. Title.
GT4985 .C37 2013
394.2663 --dc23

Second Edition

DEDICATION

This book is dedicated to:
Ann McRae Kennady Capehart (Mom)
Albert Cowardin Capehart, Sr. (Pop)
and
the ten thousand visitors who sat on SANTA AL's lap.

CONTENTS

ACKNOWLEDGEMENTS

Inking words on paper is a solo process, but it's not done alone. I want to acknowledge and thank the following folks.

First, Carolyn Renee "CR" Townsend, my wife, who in the process of helping me became Elf Renee. My mentor, coach and friend Marjorie Hudson; writing instructor Melissa Delbridge; my inspirational "writing buddy" Michele Tracy Berger; and Jane Dunlap for copyediting, publishing and IT support and who now has become Elf Helen. The First Thursday writers' support group, my writing family: Daphne Hill, Whitney Schmidt, Heather Thomas, Barb Vogel, Carol Phillips, and Patty Cole. Others who have helped move this project forward include my son, AC Capehart; his wife, Carolyn Marie Fay; faculty, colleagues and friends in the Central Carolina Community College Creative Writing Certificate Program; and fellow students in Hudson's Kitchen Table Writers' classes and workshops.

I also acknowledge my fellow Triangle Santa Buddies, the Long Leaf Pine Santas, the Virginia Santas, the School-4Santa, and the Claus Fest conferences. And finally, thanks to the Spirit for the coincidence of serendipitous events that seem to happen as the result of intent.

FOREWORD

Some men parade through life like arrogant peacocks, others stumble from day to day not sure where their life is going or even where it has been. I met Al Capehart in November 2009 when I attended my first meeting of the Triangle Santa Buddies. While I was a bit intimidated by the group of Santas I saw Al as a man who leads from his heart, and I have attempted to learn from his lead for several years.

As a storyteller who loves to share the secrets of Christmas, I have had the opportunity to work with Al on one occasion. Inside the red suit was a man who truly is Santa Claus sharing his heart and time with all who had requests of the Magic of Christmas. Beyond the red suit is a man of conviction who shares the truths of his life and beliefs not by preaching but by example. Saint Nicholas instructs every one of his Woodsmen, I am the thirteenth, to "share your life without expectation." My experiences with Al show him to be the personification of these words.

While camping at the Virginia Santa Gathering several years ago, SANTA AL and I were talking about beards. I admitted I grew my beard because I did not want to look at myself in the mirror every morning. Al's reply has lived with me every time I pass a mirror, "Why, when I look into the mirror, Santa smiles back." Yes, and Santa smiles beyond the mirror to every life fortunate enough to come into contact with this man of magical faith, determination, and inspiration.

SANTA AL presents essays about his "Santa Services" for all to read and learn from. Through these glimpses into Al's "business" and life stories we get to visit with a man who strives daily to live up to the magic he carries in his heart. Those who would be Santa, or ever wondered what it might be like to wear the red suit, can walk with a real-bearded Santa and truly feel the joy, the heartache, the wonder, the fatigue and the magic associated with this work. Through the generosity spread through these stories any reader can find the reality of being Santa, for Santa is not just the red suit we see in the malls at Christmastide but the spirit of caring, loving, and sharing throughout the year.

Al Capehart does not strut like a peacock nor does he stumble looking for his way; Al presents himself quietly with purpose, honesty and a sincere love of those fortunate to be part of his life. However, I take exception to expression of his work as "SANTA AL's Santa Services." I take exception because as I have come to know this man, and reading in his works we find the answer is "Yes, Virginia" — and Todd and Mike and Sarah and Susan and Bill and Jimmy and Rachel and children of all ages from two to one-hundred-and-two. Yes, Santa is real and he lives abundantly in the heart of this humble man in Pittsboro, North Carolina, who we know and love as SANTA AL.

E. Gale Buck, SANTA'S WOODSMAN
Author of *The Woodsman's Tale,* 2010;
Finding Nicholas, 2011;
The Secret Stories of Santa, 2012

INTRODUCTION

Part of what makes us human is the satisfaction we get from giving. It is part of our human survival function. The sense of personal satisfaction in giving comes from an endorphin surge we experience when giving. Sharing is an essential behavior in our survival. Anonymous gift giving is its highest form. Jesus, in Matthew 6:4, tells about the reward in secret gift giving. He says give "so that your giving may be in secret. And your Father who sees in secret will reward you."

Christmas cheer is part and parcel of the joy of giving, a celebration of sharing by sharing. Santa Claus is a cultural manifestation of that secret gift giving rooted in the legends of the fourth century church bishop, Saint Nicholas of Myra.

The character Santa Claus is an American invention based in historical fact, evolved by imagination, stimulated by cultural needs and always expanding. New stories appear about how some unlikely character, like a misfit reindeer with a shiny nose, saves Christmas by helping Santa Claus make his annual global run of secret gift giving. His magical visit releases the power of belief in the presence of the Christmas Spirit. Santa Claus is real, just as real as love and generosity.

Now, after decades of Santa Claus work, I've come to realize and appreciate the only gift I can give as SANTA AL is myself: my love, care and concern for all of Santa's visitors.

Santa Claus Calls Al

It all began with the beard.

I had felt a call before — to the ministry — in high school and most of the way through Duke's Divinity school. But this was different.

I was living in Durham, North Carolina, running my own handyman business: Handy Persons Associates (HPA): "No job too small. Personal attention with pride in quality." I was on the road of recovery from a devastating divorce and too much alcohol, and was living with the woman who became my third wife. For ten years I had been commuting to Raleigh on my Honda 750 motorcycle. When I finished my Ph.D. at North Carolina State University at the age of 49, I was the oldest graduate in the class of 1987.

What called me then was my new passion for turning old rail beds into bicycle paths and greenway trails, "rail-trails." HPA paid my bills and helped fund my statewide Rail-Trail volunteer organizing efforts. And, I was always looking for work. I needed the income.

Back to the beard.

In March of 1992 I stopped shaving. I'd planned a July European train tour with my son Albert Cameron (AC) to celebrate his college graduation. I wanted the convenience of not shaving while traveling. I had a beard for the trip, and decided to keep it. By October, I had grown more than two inches of grey facial hair.

Suddenly, Santa Claus began to speak to me through my customers. One customer simply started calling me "Santa." And a longtime Duke Forest customer said, "You would make a great Santa Claus. You are thoughtful. You look like Santa. You should go to the mall. See if they will hire you to play Santa."

I had not thought of myself as a Santa Claus. My father (I called him "Pop") had been a backup Santa in the 1970s and 80s for the department store he worked for in Richmond, VA. Pop loved it. Maybe my customers were on to something. At least I could go to the malls and see if they saw what my customers saw. I felt encouraged.

In early October I went to the Northgate Mall office, introduced myself, and asked about Santa Claus work. The Marketing Director said, "You do look like Santa. Here is the phone number for our Santa Set Coordinator. Give her a call."

A few days later, I met with the Coordinator. She looked me over, then handed me a Santa jacket, pants, hat, belt, gloves and black spats to cover my street shoes. She directed me to get dressed. I felt strange putting on the suit.

Would I have the Santa Claus look?

She took her three-year-old daughter and me upstairs to the mall's center court Merry Go Round. She posed us. Her daughter had a smile of delight as she looked up at me. I looked into the camera with a big grin.

After several photographs, the coordinator led us all back downstairs. She took the Santa Claus suit and said, "We'll give you a call." I waited with anticipation; the call never came.

Encouraged by Northgate's interest in my "Santa look," I applied to both South Square Mall in Durham and Cary Town Center Mall. They each signed me up for part time Santa gigs. I was excited and pleased. The hourly pay for mall Santa Claus work was more than I charged for my skilled handyman services. The timing was good, too. My handyman work slacked off during the winter months, and Santa Claus would help me make it to the spring.

I learned some things right away. I learned that most often the mall Santa is a sub-contractor to the photo company who has contracted with the mall to operate the Santa Set. Often the mall will request the photo company to contract with a specific Santa. At South Square I was an employee of the mall. But Cary Town Center contracted with Santa Plus, Inc., to run their Santa set. Santa Plus was a division of Qualex, a Kodak Company out of Missouri.

With the help of the Santa Plus "Santa Manual" I learned the basics of mall Santa Claus work. It listed professional Santa dos and don'ts and helpful hints on how to interact with children and adult visitors. It included advice about where to place your hands, how to be jolly when waving to passersby, laughter, smiles, and how to voice "Ho, Ho, Ho!" And the manual directly advised, "Don't make promises."

Instructions also warned where not to scratch, prohibited chewing tobacco and gum, and reminded me to trim my nose hairs. A child sitting on Santa's lap and looking up is looking up his nose. I followed the manual and watched other Santas. My on-the-job training experience began to shape my Santa Claus character.

In my early days I thought I'd found a mistake in the manual. It said the seventh reindeer was "Donner." I knew it to be Donder, "Thunder" in German. Blitzen is lighting. Later I learned Donner is Dutch for Thunder and is seldom used. Gene Autry's memorable 1949 rendition of *Rudolph, the Red Nosed Reindeer* reinforces the use of Donner.

Excited and pleased, I felt thankful and challenged by the "call" to the mall Santa Claus work. I began to see that it was a call to experience the joys and demands of interviewing visitors about their Christmas wishes. It was a call to smile like Santa Claus. It was a call to work with the Santa set crews, photo companies and mall management. It was a call to spread the magic of Christmas Cheer.

The real and frustrating challenge for me was to stay in character. It was hard to practice the patience required to smile while trying to delicately restrain a screaming 20-month-old for his first Santa Claus picture. I believe a big part of Santa's job is to remind folks of the magic of Christmas, to help them rekindle their belief in the power of the spirit of love and generosity, to have their childhood hearts made glad. As a real-bearded Santa, staying in character became a full time job: a mindful public presence that changes the man in — and out of — the suit.

The malls supplied the Santa suits and accessories (including the wigs and beards, which I did not need). South Square's suits were the best in the business from the renowned Santa Claus suit and accessories company, Santa & Co., LLC, St. Clair, Michigan. Their classic custom-tailored suits featured French white rabbit fur trim and full collars.

The suit assigned to me was tight across the shoulders and the sleeves were too short, but to buy one of my own was out of the question. Each of the "Super Professional" suits used by the mall cost over $1,000 in the Santa & Co. catalogue. Now I own three of these suits.

My first year working as a Santa Claus I dressed in the mall's suit, was guided by the Santa Plus manual and other Santas, and learned by doing. I didn't wear the spats. I wore the black cowboy boots I used for motorcycle riding. Fur trim around the boot tops helped, but I did get comments about being a cowboy Santa.

On Thursday, November 26, 1992, I was amazed to open the newspaper to see Northgate Mall's Thanksgiving advertising insert. The front page featured me and the Coordinator's daughter on the merry-go-round's white horse. I was taken aback by the transformation the Santa suit had made. The man on the carousel was Santa Claus. I did not see Al. I had become SANTA AL, and it took seeing that print ad to show me who I had become. Santa was saying to me, "Come on son, you can do this."

In that moment, my self-perception changed and a new path in my life was revealed. My life changed. To this day I do not market myself as Santa Claus. I can't claim to be Santa Claus. I offer Santa Claus services.

Santa is the jolly old elf, the secret gift giver on the night before Christmas, the toy maker. Santa gladdens the heart of childhood. He spreads good cheer and promotes the Christmas Spirit. He exemplifies care for those in trouble, the less fortunate, and especially children. Santa visits during the shortest days and longest nights of the year to bring hope and encouragement for a new year. This is Santa's magic. These days my business card reads, "Santa Claus Services by SANTA AL Capehart, Ph.D."

After decades of Santa Claus work, I know Santa's job is to help folks continue to believe and have hope. I think belief is a source of action. To believe in the Christmas Spirit makes it a spirit to be shared. Sharing it makes more of it. To believe in Santa Claus is to make him real. Santa becomes a living myth, a legend in touch with everything, through the Spirit of Christmas. He asks to hear your Christmas wishes. Believing in Santa Claus helps in the celebration and joy of the season. I believe Christmas gifts are really birthday gifts commemorating the birthday of Jesus Christ.

Sometimes a child will ask, "Are you real, Santa Claus?"

I pull one of their ears and ask, "Is this a real ear?"

"Yes," the youngster replies.

Then I take the child's hand, gently guide it over my big white beard and ask, "Is this a real beard?" Most say, "Yes." Some say, "No." They think it's fake. I invite the doubters to give my beard a little tug. It does not come off.

"Ouch," I say, "That hurts. It is real. Now you know Santa Claus is real."

I never got that promised call from Northgate Mall. I never got paid for modeling with the little girl on the carousel. I never went to the mall to request payment for their unauthorized use of my image. However, seeing that SANTA AL ad in the newspaper launched my Santa Claus business career. It proved to me that in the Santa suit I really do look like Santa Claus. Looking like Santa causes me to act like Santa. My life was transformed in that moment, and I'm grateful. I took the call.

CHRISTMAS PAST

From an early age I knew Santa Claus was real. When I was a boy we lived in Richmond, Virginia, half a block from Gambles Hill Park, which overlooked the James River falls. Christmas started at our house when Pop got out his train boards and miniature village. I always helped with the layout. As a four-year-old, I was opening the orange Lionel boxes that held individually wrapped rolling stock nestled in layers of tissue paper. I felt I was opening early gifts: the rust red caboose, splotchy silver Sunoco tankers, black gondolas, grey timber cars, and the magnificent black Pacific Type (4-6-2) locomotive and whistle tender.

On December 7, 1941, we were getting ready for Christmas by unpacking last Christmas. Pop tacked down the three-rail tracks in a lopsided figure 8 pattern. Our live Christmas tree would stand in the larger loop, the village in the smaller. Christmas music on the Philco radio stopped for alarming news: a Japanese sneak attack on Pearl Harbor,

Hawaii. The news brought a mood shift in our family. Our country was at war – World War II. After that Christmas, the trains went into storage and were not unpacked again until the Christmas of 1946, after Pop got home from the Navy.

In 1948 I was ten years old when our longtime live-in housekeeper, maid and cook we called "Aunt Millie" showed me gaily-wrapped packages in the back of the big closet in my parents' bedroom. Aunt Millie said, "You know, don't you, your parents are really Santa Claus?" I hadn't thought about it. So what if my folks had Christmas packages in their closet? Did that make them Santa Claus? I got gifts from both my parents and Santa Claus.

That year Santa left me a red 26-inch bicycle. The tag said, "To: Little Al From: Santa Claus." Coming down the steps and around the tall, lit Christmas tree, I saw the bicycle in the middle of the front room. I nearly leapt from the landing to the bottom step. It was beautiful. I was so excited. It had shiny black wall tires, bright rims and Bendix coaster brakes. I had already learned how to ride a two-wheeler from the kids in the neighborhood. I spent Christmas vacation mastering my bicycle. The kids and I built a ramp in the back alley and did jumps.

In January I turned eleven. I was old enough to sell newspapers. Mom and I rode the streetcar downtown to the *Richmond Times-Dispatch (RTD)* newspaper office, where I signed up to be a morning newspaper carrier. Santa knew back in December I would need a bicycle if I were to go to work as a paperboy. Santa gives useful and needed gifts.

During the week I rode my bicycle to carry my route of 89 newspapers. But the Sunday newspapers were way too thick and heavy for my bicycle. They half filled the huge trunk of Pop's dark green 1941 Chrysler New Yorker. He helped me deliver the papers to the front doors and apartments on The Boulevard. After the morning's work we rewarded ourselves with a hamburger breakfast at the White Tower restaurant on the southwest corner of Broad Street at The Boulevard.

When I turned twelve I was old enough to join Mr. Pat Brown's Boy Scout Troop #35. I became a Tenderfoot. We met downtown in the basement of our family's church, Centenary Methodist on Grace Street. I paid my dues and bought my uniform with my paperboy money. I'd had a year's experience selling, delivering and collecting, paying my bills, and had money in the bank. I was an independent sub-contractor.

Pop always said, "Pay yourself first" and had me put half of my weekly earnings into my savings account at Farmers and Merchants Bank. I usually deposited $5 to $6. My savings paid for my Boy Scout travel adventures to California, New Mexico and Canada. It had all started with a useful gift from Santa Claus.

Santa was real in my life. Gifts from Santa were helping me grow. He gave me a bicycle in preparation for going to work, earning money, and learning responsibility. The next year he gave me a change maker, a portable metal coin dispenser that I wore on my belt. It helped speed up my collecting. Useful gifts.

For six years I carried the newspaper on the same Monument Avenue route from the foot of the Matthew Fontaine Maury monument, the Confederate Path Finder of the Seas, to one block west of the General Stonewall Jackson monument. I delivered to fourteen three-story apartment buildings and four homes. My paper route money also helped Santa buy additional Lionel Train accessories.

Over the years the train set grew. In his retirement, Pop's train boards filled half of his basement. His landscape included a mountain with a train tunnel, trees, a farm, a busy village, a mirror lake and switches to his rail yard. Some afternoons he would go down to the basement to do the laundry and "play" with his trains. They carried him off on magical travels into a fanciful imaginary world. My son inherited Pop's trains, including the big transformer, track and rolling stock I had bought with my paperboy money: my gifts to Pop from Santa.

After serving in the U.S. Navy, where Pop trained ship-bound cooks, he worked in department-store retail and food service. He helped to develop and manage "the largest and finest delicatessen between New York City and Miami" (according to Mr. Charles Thalhimer, whose family owned a chain of department stores in the mid-South). From the flagship store in Richmond, Virginia, Pop shipped his special "Thalhimers Virginia Hams" all over the world as distinctive and special gifts. He could smell or taste a cheese, tell what kind it was, where it was from and perhaps in which French cave it had aged. He could squeeze a ham and tell how much fat was on it.

I never visited Santa as a child. I had heard about it from friends. Occasionally during the Christmas season Thalhimers would ask Pop to fill in as their Santa. A 1972 photograph shows Pop in his Santa suit, his custom beard hanging off his ears, his big smile, an extra-large Thalhimers shopping bag in his broad hands and tears of joy in his eyes. He loved Christmas. He loved being Santa Claus. He loved joking with the visitors and kids. He loved funny stories, jokes and puns, and children. He'd go out of his way to help anyone. Aunt Millie was right: Pop was Santa Claus.

Pop was in good company in Richmond. Across Sixth Street from Thalhimers was its archrival department store, Miller & Rhoads. Miller & Rhoads was noted for its Tea Room and its Santa. For years its Santa was the famous retired Hollywood stunt man Bill Strother. He made his entrance from a chimney. He welcomed visitors by name to his lap by the use of a concealed throat mike worn by an assistant. It took him two hours to put on his Santa face with specially designed Max Factor cosmetics and costume beard. He was considered "the most realistic-looking department-store Santa Claus." He drew large crowds of shoppers to the store. Strother, a historically significant Santa, began his career in the mid-1940s. In 2010 he was posthumously inducted into the Santa Claus Hall of Fame at the Candy Castle in Santa Claus, Indiana.

These days at our house, after all the Christmas presents from family and friends have been opened, there will be useful gifts like soap, hand tools, gloves, or a new toothbrush, all tagged, "From: Santa Claus." Santa gives useful and thoughtful gifts. Just as love and generosity are real, I believe Santa Claus is real. Now, forty years after Pop's Santa photo was taken, when I put on my Santa face I look in the mirror. I see my father's smile, his twinkling blue eyes, and feel I'm looking at Santa Claus. Santa winks at me. I smile and wink back. I know the real Santa Claus. I see him every day.

Becoming Santa Al

Becoming SANTA AL starts on the inside. Most folks don't know how a Santa day begins behind the scenes. Here is how one of my days as a working Santa starts. I think of it as a walking meditation into the work ahead.

It is still dark Saturday morning of the third week of my thirteenth Holiday Season working as a mall Santa Claus. I roll out of my warm bed, have my tea, wash out my sinuses with my Neti Pot saline solution, and read the morning newspapers (especially the editorial cartoons and the comics). I tug on my red sweats and go to the chilly garage studio and practice yoga for 50 minutes. I stretch into the Warrior and the Triangle poses to realign my hips and pelvis, already stressed this early in the season from the squirming weight of heavy children and adults on my lap.

In the shower, I use Pantene Silver Expressions shampoo and conditioner to lighten my beard, bleached to a consistent white. Pantene Curly Mousse helps with control and lift, then a squirt of hair spray holds my ample beard in place. I apply Schwarzkopf got2b glued styling gel to my mustache, twisting it into a curly smile, and to my eyebrows, sculpted to suggest a windswept, elfin look. I use a hair dryer to set the mousse and glue. I carefully pull an REI moisture-wicking undershirt over my head, step into clean white boxer shorts, and adjust my Gold Toe compression socks to help with circulation and lower leg swelling. Jeans, sneakers, a flannel-lined plaid shirt, a down vest, and my signature white porkpie hat (to cover my fearsome frontal lobe) complete my "traveling" attire.

I pack my grub cache for the 14-hour day ahead: breakfast soup of 2 cups watered-down powdered milk, oatmeal, honey, raisins and chopped pecans in a 32-ounce Brown Cow yogurt container; 2 whole wheat peanut butter with strawberry preserves sandwiches; a banana; a large handful of toasted almonds in a Ziploc bag; and 5 bottles of water. I need to keep my strength up and be well hydrated to make it through the day.

My sleigh is a silver Toyota Sienna All Wheel Drive (just in case of snow) minivan. On the front tag is an image of a reindeer named Comet. The van has sleek red racing stripes widening from the front fenders to the back, giving the impression of a sleigh in motion. Sculptured letters advertise www.santaal.com below the racing stripe on the back hatch. The bumper says "HO! HO! HO!" Because I do not drive to gigs in my Santa Claus suit, Comet is my dressing room, with make-up, props, suits and a full-length nap space with blanket, pillow and a cat eye propane heater.

Leaving my gravel driveway, I look up at the historic Chatham County Courthouse clock tower in the middle of Pittsboro's downtown traffic circle. It's 8:30 a.m. Comet needs to land in the back parking lot of Crabtree Valley Mall in Raleigh by 9:25. The traffic flow is good and we arrive at 9:15.

I finish my breakfast and wash down my dietary supplements. I park in my usual spot on the first level, in the middle of the mall, opposite the set of double glass doors opening to the Center Court. I park facing out over Crabtree Creek and its inviting greenway trail, a legacy from one of my greenway trails colleagues. I'd love to bicycle it today, but the Santa Claus work takes all of my time.

The final change takes place in Comet. My three professional grade suits are from Santa & Co. in St. Clair, Michigan. One is for outdoors and parades; one for home visits, the mall and public events; and the best one for country clubs and commercials. Because I have other gigs today, I have two suits with me, leaving one at home to assure a back up if Comet is broken into. I brush my teeth and lay out the mall suit. I spray the palms of my white gloves with pine-scented cologne and fold them together. As I step into the red wool, satin-lined knicker Santa pants, I pray:

Oh, Lord God, Heavenly Father, help Santa Claus to share in and spread the Christmas Spirit in the celebration of the birthday of Your Son, Our Lord Jesus Christ, the Prince of Peace. Amen.

Then, like a firefighter, I slip over my shoulders the two-inch wide red Vermont Country Store suspenders already clipped to the pants. I roll up my street clothes and stuff them against the van's wall. I slip the gloves into the right front pocket.

Now I pull on the fur-trimmed Santa boots: black square-toed Civil War Reenactment infantry boots custom-built by Crescent City Sutler in Evansville, Indiana. Using my high school Cadet Corps and Navy shoeshine experience, I keep the boots clean and polished. They have arch support inserts, and two-toned sleigh bells attached to the back next to the pull straps almost under the fur. They make musical jingles when I walk.

For good luck in warding off children's germs, I swallow a cup of Airborne immune-boosting strawberry-flavored fizzy water. Now I'm ready for the makeup. I work white makeup paste into my beard on my chin and skin under my lower lip. Without this cover up the camera's flash will reflect shiny skin between the whiskers, my lip and chin. I brush white mascara into my bleached eyebrows to give them an arch to look wind swept and frosty from driving the sleigh in winter weather.

Eye drops brighten and clear my eyes. Lip balm adds a sheen to my lips and a shine to my smile. In September I began my teeth-whitening program. They're looking good. I rub a drop of patchouli oil into each cheek, a pungent woodsy fragrance for those who get close. For some, it smells of Bay Rum, just like "dear old Daddy." Then I lightly apply rouge to my cheeks and nose, for as the well-known poem says,

His eyes — how they twinkled!
His dimples: how merry,
His cheeks were like roses, his nose like a cherry.

A final check in the mirror: Santa Claus's face has appeared.

The frame for this look will be my red jacket trimmed in white fur, big black belt, and fur-trimmed hat with its jester's ball. I think of Santa's hat as a soft bishop's mitre, a latter-day version of the bishop's pointed mitre for the "jolly old elf."

In preparation to don the jacket I pull on glove extenders. The extenders are my invention. They cover my forearm between the end of the short white gloves and the beginning of the jacket's red elastic cuff lining, which slides halfway to my elbow when I wave. My wife made the extenders from white two-way stretchy material sewn into a 12-inch long wrist-size tube with a thumbhole. The extenders give a clean, crisp and professional appearance, and free my hand and arm movements for waving without concern about revealing my hairy arms. I want only my "Santa face" to show.

I prepare for the Santa hat by tying a large red patterned bandana around my head. The bandana will act as a sweatband between my head and the satin-lined, fur-trimmed hat. I pause and pray for wisdom and insight.

O Lord, I pray for wisdom to listen, insight in under-
standing, to speak with knowledge and to express care
and love in the Spirit of Saint Nicholas.

I check and load my pants pockets. My wallet with SANTA AL's business cards go in the left rear pocket with its button-down flap. In the right front are my Spartan Swiss Army pocket knife, 3 honey-lemon cough drops and my freshly scented white gloves. Comet's key is in the left front pocket, with a clean white folded handkerchief and a full 16-ounce water bottle.

After a half an hour, I'm almost ready. I put on my crystal clear half-eye readers with my trademark red string. I slip the satin-lined red wool jacket over my moisture-wicking T-shirt. My Santa belt is four and a half inches wide, black patent leather with an oversized aluminum buckle and hidden snaps. It slides through the two belt loops on the jacket and goes around my tummy, not my waist. The belt reminds me of my motorcycle riding and weight lifting days when I used a kidney belt. The belt helps support my back for the seated working position. And, it gets sweaty hot.

Finally, I carefully place the hat on my head, making sure the bandana doesn't show. The hat has an adjustable crown inside to make sure it is not too high or too low on my head. I pull it two fingers above my eyebrows. Being right-handed, I usually wear the ball on my left. The hat's ball is the classic length and nearly comes to my shoulder. This keeps it out of the way for visitors who mostly perch on my right thigh. When I cradle infants in my left arm, the ball becomes an attraction for their tiny fingers.

I look in the mirror. Santa smiles back at me.

Now for two more props: the 3 rich-sounding sleigh

bells on a leather cuff just long enough to slip over my left wrist, and my dog-eared copy of the Random House Pictureback edition of *The Night Before Christmas* illustrated by Douglas Grosline. I particularly like Grosline's centerfold illustration, a beautiful and realistic artwork of the eight reindeer flying toward the snow-covered rooftop, pulling Santa and his toy-filled sleigh. The bright, full moon shines in a starry night sky over the snow-covered town. A brilliant Star of Bethlehem lights the horizon.

When visitors ask, "Where are your reindeer?" SANTA AL will say, "Oh, you know the reindeer? Do you know Dasher, Dancer, Prancer, Vixen, Comet, Cupid, Donder and Blitzen?" He will open the book and point them out in Grosline's illustration of the prancing reindeer flying toward the chimney.

"But Santa, where is Rudolph, the red-nosed reindeer?"

Santa will reply with a question, "When does Santa Claus need Rudolph? Rudolph guides Santa's sleigh on foggy Christmas Eves." He will invite the visitor to look at the illustration again. "With the light from the full moon and stars, there is no need for Rudolph. He is a specialized reindeer."

My transformation to SANTA AL is almost complete.

I lock Comet and walk toward the mall's entrance. Crossing four lanes of parking garage traffic and the mall's circular street, I pull on my white gloves and imagine myself going to work like a cowboy. My boots' bells ring out my presence and alert children and adults that Santa is coming. I wave and greet folks with "Merry Christmas,

Ho, Ho, Ho!"

The path to the Santa Photo Set is about 120 yards through the double doors past Panera Bread, Crate and Barrel, other shops, and Dunkin' Donuts (where Santa will later take his break.) I shake hands with folks as I pass, leaving behind smiles and an aroma of the piney north woods. Occasionally someone asks, "Can I have a hug, Santa?" or "Can I tell you what I want for Christmas?" A brief exchange usually ends with a little hug, soft chuckles and a wish for a "Merry Christmas!" I try to allow time for these personal encounters on the way to the big green and white Santa chair.

I enter the Santa Photo Set through the exit, drop off my props and water bottle at the chair and switch on the floor fan, cleverly hidden in a large box wrapped to look like a giant present. The fan helps dissipate my body heat from the suit. I go to the visitors' line and greet everyone who is waiting there. Then I invite the first visitors to come in, saying, "Let's go sit in the 'Big Chair' so you can tell Santa Claus what you want for Christmas."

It is 10 a.m. The transformation is complete. The Spirit of Christmas is now working through me. SANTA AL will be spinning his Santa Claus Magic late into the night.

CHRISTMAS GIFT

The Santa Claus Oath says

I understand that the true and only gift I can give,
as Santa, is myself.

People ask Santa for all kinds of gifts. He provides an opportunity to believe, to release your "kid power" to make-believe. In laughter, joy and love, Santa gives hugs and Ho, Ho, Hos. He embodies the Spirit of Christmas. In legend, he grants wishes, gives gifts and blessings. I love the Santa Claus work. I help to bring the Christmas Spirit by sharing it. By sharing the spirit, I feel it, too.

The spirit of Santa Claus is real. You recognize Santa's spirit and presence by his hat alone, as he rings a bell over the red Salvation Army kettle, encouraging generosity in charity. He partners with Toys-for-Tots drives, helping to make sure that every child gets a gift for Christmas. He is an inspiration for the recent Secret Santa movement, where strangers pay for toys that a struggling Mom or Dad has put on lay-a-way. The customers learn when they come to get the toys that a Secret Santa has already paid for them. Secret gift giving, the highest form of giving, is exemplified in the legend of St. Nicholas, where the recipient does not know the giver and the giver does not know the recipient.

Santa Claus is a mysterious presence, a living legend. He visits your house on the night before Christmas to leave gifts. He has magical powers of flying reindeer, secret entry, knows your wishes, your behavior: whether you are naughty or nice. You see Santa at the end of the Thanksgiving Day Parade, get your picture with him at the shopping mall, or maybe you're with him at a holiday party. But you never see Santa Claus on Christmas Eve, when he visits your house!

Santa's appearance in malls and parades signals it's time to get ready: the holiday season is coming and the Christmas Spirit is on its way. Part of the fun in my Santa Claus work is being that messenger wishing "Merry Christmas and Happy New Year!" To hear the greeting returned lifts my spirits. The exchanged greeting with friends and strangers builds community by sharing the anticipation and blessings of Christmas and the opportunities in a new year. The more it is shared, the more there is to share.

Often we see what we are looking for. As the holiday season gets close, folks — especially children — start looking for Santa Claus. During the season people often recognize me as Santa Claus, even in my street clothes. I will sometimes overhear a parent say to a child while looking at me, "I think I see Santa Claus." The bushy white beard, twinkly blue eyes, big tummy, the fat-cheeked smile, ready chuckles and laughter, are all a part of who I am. Sometimes I feel the spirit of Santa Claus comes out through me. I always try to be mindful of who I may appear to be.

On a shuttle bus between the NC State Fair and satellite parking in Cary, my wife and I sat near the back exit. As a mother and daughter were leaving, they passed behind me. The mother leaned over my shoulder and whispered, "My daughter thinks you are Santa Claus, disguised in ordinary person clothes." I gave her a SANTA AL business card, saying, "Tell her she is right. She is a clever girl to have recognized Santa. And remind her to continue to be good. Ho, Ho, Ho!" She smiled and gave her daughter a little hug as they stepped off the bus.

As SANTA AL, I do Santa Claus work, but I don't claim to be Santa Claus.

Adults may miss Santa Claus where children often find him. What do the children see? A white-bearded, kindly old grandfather with a smile? What do the adults see? A glaring, staring, dirty old man? I try to be aware of the images being projected onto me as I carry forward the Santa Claus work.

In the grocery store after Thanksgiving, as I walked down the aisle toward the bread section, I saw a young girl about six years old standing next to her dad, who leaned over the beer cases examining the boutique beers. As I approached, she looked up, smiled and said, "Hi!"

I winked, smiled, and asked, "Have you been being good?"

"Yes, sir," she replied.

"Then I'll see you soon," I said.

Her dad looked up to see me going down the aisle, looked down at his daughter and asked, "Do you know that old man?" He had missed the Santa in the old man. She had seen the Santa. We see what we believe.

The father would have recognized Santa Claus in his red suit. The sudden and bright presence of Santa Claus in his full regalia is a gift to the viewer, a presence as a present. Young children often see Santa's spirit even without the traffic-light-red clothing. Because they believe in Santa, they look and see what others can't. They see what those who don't believe can't see.

At the Celebrate Santa Convention in Gatlinburg, Tennessee, in March 2009, six hundred other Santas and I said and signed the Santa Oath in its first national ceremony. Santa Phillip Wenz composed it. Since 1989, SANTA PHIL has been the Santa Claus of Santa's Village Park in East Dundee, Illinois, west of Chicago. He and other Santa brotherhoods promote the oath worldwide from Santa Claus, Indiana, "America's Christmas Hometown."

For me, the Santa Oath spells out the mystery in Santa's mission. It helps my understanding and commitment to the Santa Claus work, especially the notion that the only gift I have to give is myself.

The Santa Oath

I, (SANTA AL) will seek knowledge to be well versed in the mysteries of bringing Christmas cheer and good will to all the people that I encounter in my journeys and travels. I shall be dedicated to hearing the secret dreams of both children and adults. I understand that the true and only gift I can give, as Santa, is myself.

I acknowledge that some of the requests I will hear will be difficult and sad.

I know in these difficulties there lies an opportunity to bring a spirit of warmth, understanding and compassion. I know the "real reason for the season" and know that I am blessed to be able to be a part of it. I realize that I belong to a brotherhood and will be supportive, honest and show fellowship to my peers.

I promise to use "my" powers to create happiness, spread love and make fantasies come to life in the true and sincere tradition of the Santa Claus legend. I pledge myself to these principles as a descendant of Saint Nicholas, the gift giver of Myra.

For centuries folks have recognized and known Santa Claus. When I visit with older folks I remind them they have known Santa all their lives. Santa can help folks to become Santa Claus for themselves, by giving them permission to do good things for themselves and encouragement to follow their dreams.

One day, back when computers were becoming a necessary part of business and contemporary life, I was returning to a mall's Santa set, when a professionally dressed, middle-aged African-American woman approached me.

She said, "Santa, I wanted to tell you what I want for Christmas."

I paused, faced her, smiled and said, "Yes, Sweetheart, tell Santa Claus what you want for Christmas." (I call all women and girls "Sweetheart" and all boys and men "Son").

She said, "Santa, I want a computer."

"Yes," I said, "Computers have become very popular and important in today's world." I asked, "Do you have a place for your computer?"

"No," she said.

"Well," I said, "first you have to make a place for your computer to land. When you make a space for it in your life, your computer will come."

"Okay," she said, "I'll make a place for it. Thanks, Santa. I knew I was talking to a wise old man." I gave her a little embrace and wished her Merry Christmas.

During another season, while working in a small mall with a basic Santa set, a young mom approached with her two young sons. Her boys climbed onto my lap, shared their wish lists and got their $5 photo. As they were leaving, the mom leaned over to me and said, "Santa, what I need for Christmas is a bigger house. My family is growing, but my husband doesn't want to move."

I asked, "Do you have a particular neighborhood in mind?"

"Yes," she said, "I have two I'm interested in."

I suggested she drive those neighborhoods to see what was for sale and what interested her, then select two to show to her husband. "Get your husband to go for a ride with you 'just to look'." She said she would give it a try. I gave her a smile, we shared a little hug, and I wished her "Good Luck and Merry Christmas!" She left like she was on a mission.

The next year, at the same mall, one of my first visitors was the young house-hunting mother. She took my face in both of her hands, lifted my head and planted a big kiss on my forehead. She had done her homework, found two places she wanted her husband to see. He'd agreed to go to take a look. Over the Fourth of July weekend she had moved her family into a larger house in a nicer neighborhood. Her husband was sold on the freestanding garage and shop. He'd always wanted to have his own shop. Opportunity opened to her because she knew what she wanted, had asked for help, and was working to make it happen.

Santa Claus is a receiver as well as a giver. He receives the gift of those wonderful Christmas wish lists written by small children. For three- to six-year-olds, their first letter writing may be a letter to Santa. They are self-motivated, wanting to get their wish list to him. These days a Google search for "letters to Santa" pulls up online services that give instructions as to what to include in the letter, how to make sure Santa or one of his helpers gets it, and how to get a return letter.

A printed or handwritten letter with a pencil, ballpoint pen or crayon is an expression of a child's personal self. The child's aspirations become visible on paper. There may be stickers or ads for toys glued to the letter to make sure Santa knows specifically what model they want. Most lists are based on TV ads.

Many children will ask for more of the same of what they already have, like more Pokemon cards, Webkins, Zuzu pets, computer games, and always more Legos. I've had parents come back after their child's visit to retrieve the youngster's handwritten letter to Santa for the family's scrapbook. The letter to Santa becomes a historic family document.

When youngsters bring a long list, I ask them to select their top three items. In this way I lead a discussion toward what the child wants most. It helps the child then to identify the number one item on their list: what they want most of all.

After years of reviewing children's long lists, I've noticed their most desired item is often near the end. A list may start with computer games, include more Legos, and then end with a trumpet. List making is a type of self-discovery. By brainstorming and priority setting, the heart's desire begins to emerge. Once the top item is identified, there is a greater likelihood of getting it, because it is now known as "Number One." I will suggest they tell a grandparent or relative their top choice. They may be able to help Santa Claus. Just by being with and talking to Santa they come to know more about themself and what they really want.

In addition to helping set priorities and goals, I encourage good behavior. My Santa "be good" rap includes, "Do what your folks ask you to do. Get along with your brothers and sisters and friends; pick up your things, because nobody likes a mess. And remember to do good things for yourself, because part of being good is to do good things for yourself, like go to bed on time, eat your fruits and vegetables, brush your teeth, and always use your helmet when you ride a bicycle or a skateboard to protect your smart brain. Santa loves all his boys and girls and wants good things for you."

I've had youngsters curl up on my lap who don't want to leave at the end of our visit. Their parents literally had to pull them off. Listening to Santa's soothing baritone voice telling them they are loved, sitting on his soft fur-trimmed jacket, leaning into his fur-cuffed sleeves and snuggling into his arms, they feel warm, comfortable, safe and secure. When the child feels safe, loved and connected, he or she can share feelings, ideas and personal goals with Santa. Decisions are made and plans begun.

One boy wanted a drum set. We talked about the power and influence of music in our lives. We discussed the kind of music he liked. I asked, "Where can you practice?"

"Maybe in the basement," he said. I reminded him that learning to play a musical instrument takes time and lots of practice. He should ask his parents to help. "Perhaps they can pay for music lessons. Or, if you have a family member who knows the instrument, they could help you learn and practice." It is important for Santa to encourage such a child to ask for help in pursuit of his dream.

Some people think Santa Claus is a "fixer" or matchmaker. One day I was working in Santa's Magic Castle at South Square Mall in Durham and the early afternoon Santa line had dwindled to none. In the lull an attractive, well-dressed woman in her mid-30s approached the set. I looked up to see a gold Star of David riding atop her cleavage. The male mall walkers sometimes teased me about attractive women sitting on my lap. They are lovely to look at, but when one sits on my leg, she is just more dead weight on sore thighs. She walked up and sat on my left knee.

She said, "Santa, I don't believe in you, but I know you have magic powers. You can make things happen. I've come to you for help."

"Yes," I said, "Santa is known to have magic, but he doesn't display it."

She continued, "Santa, I recently moved to the Research Triangle. I need a boyfriend. Can you help me?"

"Well, Santa isn't a matchmaker," I said. "But, have you been to Temple Beth El? It's on the corner of Markham Avenue and Watts Street in the Trinity Park neighborhood."

She had heard of it, but she hadn't been. She promised to go check it out. As she left, Santa wished her a "Happy Hanukkah."

The following year — same mall, about the same time of day — the young woman appeared again at the Santa set. She looked as good as ever, her gold star in its place. Again sitting on Santa's lap, she said, "Santa, I knew you could do magic. I've met Ervin. But he needs a 'real' job. All he ever does is play the stock market."

Thinking she wanted more intimate and personal time with Ervin, I suggested, "Perhaps you need to become more interested in what Ervin is doing. As you do, you'll have more time with him and learn more about him."

Getting up to leave, she said, "Well, I might give it a try." She left without thanking me for helping her find Ervin in the first place. But it proves Santa's magic. All you have to do is ask and believe.

Santa Claus can give blessings and prayers.

Often I hold an infant in my arms as the parents and grandparents gather about the big digital camera to select the perfect picture. Infants don't come with long wish lists. I usually take advantage of my personal time with the child by giving a blessing. I developed what I call the "Saint Nicholas Blessing." I gently place my gloved hand on the infant's head, trying not to frighten the child. I say:

Santa Claus as Saint Nicholas blesses you, Bonnie, that you may grow in health, wisdom and prosperity to help bring peace to the earth as we prepare to celebrate the birthday of the Prince of Peace. You are one of Santa's good girls. Santa Claus loves you.

Parents who overhear the blessing sometimes tear up. Some return the following year and ask for the blessing again. I don't know if any of these babies are baptized, but the Saint Nicholas Blessing is my way of blessing them.

Sometimes a visitor – an adult or a child – will ask me to pray for them. When I'm asked to pray, I offer to pray with my visitor right there. We become a prayer team, multiplying our spiritual power and effect.

One youngster asked that I pray for her grandfather who was having open-heart surgery at a regional hospital. I asked her grandfather's name. "Hoyt," she said. Holding her hands I said, "Join me in praying for your grandfather."

Almighty God, Father and Creator of all, we pray for grandfather Hoyt that he will be strong, healthy and recover quickly from his open-heart surgery. We pray for his surgeons and hospital staff that their knowledge, care and skill will cure his ailment and restore him to health. We pray for Hoyt's family, his wife and all his children and grandchildren that they may be a comfort to him by sharing their love for him and for one another. We pray thy will be done for Hoyt through Jesus Christ our Lord, Amen.

I then hugged the child, saying,

Santa Claus blesses you and your
love for your grandfather.
Peace be with you, Amen.

And sometimes Santa will offer to pray for the visitor who seems to need it. Santa Cliff Snider of High Point, NC, carries a small book full of names of kids he prays for.

Once a child asked SANTA CLIFF if he could stop a bully. He told the child to tell his teacher, and then, in the presence of the boy, added his name to Santa's book, telling him, "Santa Claus will be praying for your safety."

Santa's presence is the gift of himself.

SANTA'S ELVES

Hanna was two and half years old when she got "Elven," her Elf on the Shelf®. When she first saw him sitting on her bedroom shelf with his little green legs and pointy shoes hanging down, she looked up at Elven's tiny pointy ears and said, "He's not real." Unlike Elf Magic Elf®, who may accompany a child in her daily activities, the Elf on the Shelf is untouchable.

The next morning when Hanna looked for Elven, he was sitting at the opposite end of the shelf with his legs crossed. Every morning Elven landed in a different spot and in a different position after returning from his overnight trip to report on Hanna's behavior to Santa Claus. With all that moving around Elven must be real, she thought, but he still looks like an elf doll. Now at seven years old, Hanna talks with Elven like a friend. He is her advocate with Santa Claus. Both she and Eric, her four-year-old little brother, have regular conversations with Elven. Their magical imaginations have made him a reality.

When the Elf on the Shelf product first appeared in 2005, I worried it was like inviting a spy in the household. A spy who you can see watching you, but who you can't touch. As described in the accompanying *The Elf on the Shelf* book, you name your elf and every night between Thanksgiving and Christmas your elf magically teleports to the North Pole to report on your behavior. The parents and grandparents I have talked to say the Elf on the Shelf has positive results in effecting desirable behavior, especially between siblings. Perhaps Santa's legendary judging and gift giving are used both as a stick and a carrot. The Elf of the Shelf is another pair of eyes "watching you," so you'd better be good.

The elves' seasonal arrival helps families prepare for Christmas. The elf brings a sense of anticipation and an awareness of a coming magical event: Christmas morning and the visit from St. Nicholas.

Elves are critical in Santa Claus' work. They explain how Santa Claus can get so much done. Elves have expanded their roles to include being Santa's agents as well as toy makers, bakers and helpers. Elves are integral to the Santa Claus mythology. America's Christmas Elves/Santa's Elves have been traced to *Little Women* author Louisa May Alcott's 1850s unpublished manuscript titled *Christmas Elves*. Alcott's elves also appear in her poetry. The 1873 Christmas cover of the popular woman's magazine *Godey's Lady's Book* depicts Santa Claus surrounded by toys and elves showing all the work and preparations necessary to supply young folks with toys at Christmas time.

In the 1994 movie *The Santa Clause,* Santa and his elves are managed by the head elf, Bernard, with assistance from Elf Judy, who is only 1200 years old.

Will Farrell starred in the 2003 movie *Elf,* in which he is raised by elves but grows to be a human-size elf. He has magical powers and spreads Christmas cheer by singing out loud for all to hear. The 2004 movie *The Polar Express* portrayed the North Pole and Santa's Village as a Northern European style city of tens of thousands of elves, the toy makers.

Elves are independent operatives, knowledgeable, and helpful, with highly developed specialty skills including toy making, cookie baking, picture taking and Santa helping. An elf can be small of stature, have an elusive presence and be a little mischievous in character, but always helpful.

Elf Renee came to help SANTA AL in 2011. My wife Carolyn Renee (CR) helped at two hometown gigs. At the first job she greeted visitors, did traffic control and passed out coloring books and other giveaways. A little girl visiting Santa wanted to know, "Where are your elves, Santa Claus?" I pointed to CR in her green pants, red and green vest and Santa Claus baseball cap, and said. "There she is. She is the Green Elf." She was satisfied. She had seen an elf.

For our second hometown gig CR bought a color ink printer for her digital camera and took pictures. A picture with Santa was part of the Santa giveaway. Like at the first gig, another little girl asked, "Where are your elves, Santa Claus?"

I pointed to CR in her green outfit and said, "There she is. She is the Green Elf."

"Yes, I can see she is green," said the little girl, "But what is her name?"

Thinking of CR's middle name, I said, "Her name is Renee, Elf Renee. She is a great help to Santa Claus. And she takes the pictures."

The little girl seemed satisfied. She had not only seen an elf, she knew the elf's name. There is power in knowing elf names.

Twenty years ago when I first started my Santa Claus work, I thought CR could help as Mrs. Claus. But she saw potential conflict between Santa and the Mrs. She said, "No! I am not a performer. I'll help where I can, but I will not be a Mrs. Claus. The role does not suit me."

She's helped from time to time with the pictures and darning the Santa suit. Elf Renee is a great Christmas name for CR. She is nearly five feet tall with fair skin, red hair, green eyes and has an aura of elfin busyness about her. At church she's coffee host, vestry clerk, serves on the altar guild, is a lay minister and lector and is active with the Episcopal Church Women. She's busy at the Senior Center, AARP, in the neighborhood, in the community, and is a volunteer advocate for nursing home residents in Chatham County. Her positive spirit of thoughtfulness and care, and of getting the job done, now, demonstrates "elfness."

For our next season I ordered a pair of custom-made, authentic, curly-toed green elf shoes with bells for CR. After all these years, she has identified her seasonal role.

She is Elf Renee. Thank you, Santa Claus. Thank you, Elf Renee.

Last season I worked the big chair in the Santa Claus tent at Raleigh's Pullen Park for the Crabtree Rotary Holiday Express Train. One night, Aimee, who looked to be six years old, came to see Santa and gave me a little red plastic bag with instructions not to open it until I got home. The note in the bag said her gift was for her Elf on the Shelf, Jerry. Not being able to touch Jerry, and knowing that he lives with me at the North Pole, she decided to give her gift to Jerry by way of Santa Claus. Santa is the secret gift giver, after all. Aimee was practicing love and generosity.

Elf Jerry got a Santa Christmas card, a tree ornament, an eraser and a slightly used red sweetheart pencil. I told Aimee, "You are a special person. Most children tell Santa the things they want to receive. But you are a very thoughtful young girl. You want to give gifts, too. You are what Santa Claus calls a gift-giving child. You are special. Santa loves you, Aimee. Merry Christmas."

Lights And Voices

Everyone came to see Santa Claus at the annual Raleigh Celebration of Lights. Bumper to bumper, in the dark with only parking lights, cars crawled along in single file, their radios tuned to the holiday music frequency that broadcasts from the visitors' center and blasts into the Santa Village. Halfway through the two-mile light show was the Santa Claus circus tent. In the middle of the set, flooded by bright stage lights, sat Santa's big green chair waiting for Santa, visitors and photos.

I worked nights there as SANTA AL for four years. When working the tent, I called SANTA AL the "Side Show Santa." All kinds of folks: kids in footed pajamas, Red Hat Society ladies, families, teens, drunks and church groups came to sit on my knee for a visit and a photo. Here are a few glimpses of those special evenings.

I've been working the chair for five hours with two five-minute breaks and have seen about 327 folks. Now the line is down to 22. The entrance gates close at 10 p.m. but the traffic continues through the exhibit for another 45 minutes. The crowds and the line of cars at the Santa Village parking lot dwindle.

My next visitor is unsteady on his feet. The Santa helper asks, "Do you want a $5 snapshot of your visit with Santa?" The visit with Santa is free.

"No," he says, "I don't want no picture. I jus' wanna talk to Santa Claus." He stumbles toward the big chair, his Pittsburgh Steelers jacket open. Unshaven, with bloodshot blue eyes, he carries a heavy odor of whiskey.

Smiling, I greet him with my usual rap about how pleased Santa Claus is that he has come to see him. Sliding back into the chair, I put my right leg next to the large plush arm of the chair, and guide him to sit on the arm. Large and wiry, he rests his weight on the chair, not my leg. I reach up and put my right hand on his shoulder and pull him in a little closer, "Tell Santa Claus what you want for Christmas."

With a cloud of whiskey breath he hesitantly says, "I - want - to - be - a - better - person."

Wow, I didn't expect that. Repeating his request to let him know I have heard him, I say, "Oh, you want to be a better person?"

"Yes, I do," he says.

I ask him, "How can you be a better person?"

Pausing and looking deeply into my face, his eyes

well up with tears as he says, "I can go see my Mom for Christmas."

Smiling slightly, I realize he has answered his own request.

"Hey," I say, "You are already a better person. You just told Santa Claus you plan to visit your mother for Christmas. Your visit will be a gift to her. And visiting her will make you a better person. She will love you for it."

I give him a manly shoulder hug, pat him strongly on his back, and help lift his elbow as he slowly steadies himself onto his wobbly legs. I say, "Merry Christmas, Happy New Year and remember, you are now a better person."

As he starts down the exit ramp, he stops, turns and looks back with tears still in his eyes but with a little smile on his face. He has told his Christmas wish to Santa Claus and with Santa's help he has made a plan on how to do it. Santa's magic can work for those who believe. Perhaps he already feels like a "better person."

For $15 a car, loaded van or church bus, folks drive through arches of flashing lights, flying cannon balls, leaping reindeer, windmills, children's storybook characters, holiday greetings and more. Darkness reveals the enchanted wonderland of lights, adding mystery and excitement to the Santa Village. It takes about an hour to cruise the entire exhibit. Off the parking lot is a small midway with a kids' "hands on" tent for making crafts, including Christmas cards and writing a letter to Santa. Vendors sell gifts, trinkets, fudge and baked goods. Across from two kiddy rides Fast Freddy pours sweet batter into hot oil, making fragrant funnel cakes. It smells like the State Fair.

Frosty's trailer stands at the tent's entrance selling the "Best Hot Chocolate in the Triangle," using real Ghirardelli chocolate. He also has hot coffee, hot cider and oven-fresh oversized pastries and cookies from Sweet Jane's Bakery in Durham. I've known Frosty since 1968; we met during the formation of the Carolina Tarwheels Bicycle Club of Durham-Chapel Hill. He owned and managed a couple of bicycle shops and now peddles the Triangle's Best Hot Chocolate. We greet each other in passing.

Visitors push through the curtain of plastic strips to enter the heated tent. To the left the kiddy train station sells tickets for the miniature rubber tire "train" ride down and back on its side-track. On the right a row of folding chairs face a giant projection screen featuring holiday videos, including the story of Rudolph the Red-Nosed Reindeer. The Café against the back wall offers hard candy and trinkets. Ahead, ropes and stanchions form a serpentine line in the large open court in front of the Santa set entrance booth. For $5 you can buy a snapshot of your visit or you can use your own camera. The visit with Santa is free.

The Santa tent has two large openings. Compared to the mall, this Santa set has primitive facilities for the comfort of Santa. Two large LP gas heaters vent into the tent's floor near the Santa set. On very cold nights I can see ice form on the inside of the tent at the top at the poles. In heavy rain, rivulets of water run under the Santa set platform and across the Café floor. Hidden behind the Santa set in the back of the tent is a small, unsecured flap. When I need a break, I tell visitors Santa will be back in five minutes, go behind the set, and slip unseen to the Port-a-John. It's the only place I can get a break on the night shift.

There's a sturdy, green, big-armed upholstered chair for Santa Claus visiting and photos. A piece of plywood under the seat cushion keeps my butt from sinking into the chair, giving a straight line from my hips to my knees directly over my feet. This position makes it possible to balance knee-sitting visitors without muscle strain. For heavy visitors I move my knees up against the arms. The visitor can stand and lean back against my straight leg, or sit on the chair arms. From the front it looks like the visitor is sitting on my lap. Adults standing behind the chair can join in a family photo.

The green Astroturf floor covering hides two different thicknesses of plywood sub-floor under the chair. The chair sits unevenly, and one night the back legs slide off the thicker plywood. I hear a crack as the legs drop down. Getting up out of the chair, and with a helper, we lift it back up and forward so all of the legs sit evenly on the thicker plywood.

The next visitors, a heavy young adult couple, sit one on each arm of the chair. As I scoot forward to get into position for the photo, the back legs of the chair break. I slide to the floor with the two heavy weights on my thighs!

What a sight, Santa Claus sitting on the floor in a broken-down chair with his legs splayed out, two big folks on his lap! I still had my hands on their backs to keep them from tipping over. Thank goodness no one was hurt. Afterwards I wished I'd had the presence of mind to ask the photographer to take a picture.

It took three days to repair the green chair. The folding chair I had to use during the repair was very uncomfortable, painful, and gave no leg support. It was hard those three days to keep up the Christmas Spirit.

The city has recently bought the North Pole Post Office Santa set from Crabtree Valley Mall to use in the Santa tent. The mall updated their Santa set to a Nutcracker Suite scene. I work both sets, the Nutcracker at the mall in the morning and the Post Office at the Walnut Creek Amphitheater at night.

To the right of the Santa chair, the Post Office wall has clocks in different time zones and a world map with a lighted red line from the North Pole directly to Raleigh, NC. Together, the walls form a 'V' at the chair for the visitor line in and out. The wall on the left has a grid of square mailboxes filled with letters to the North Pole. Stuffed animals sit on the edge of the counter at the bottom of the mailboxes. At the end of the counter are two "out boxes," one labeled Naughty, the other Nice. The Nice out box is full. The Naughty box contains only two letters.

Gold ropes and white cotton snow keep visitors on the ramps that lead to and from the Santa Chair. Behind the chair, hanging on the side of the tent, is a 12 by 15-foot snowy mountain scene backdrop. Several freshly cut and decorated North Carolina Fraser fir trees beside the chair and in front of the backdrop give off the fragrant assurance of Christmas.

The visitor traffic flow is steady tonight except when a bored kid tries to swing on the gold cord that divides the lanes. His weight pulls over the cord stanchions, which fall to the floor with a great clatter and a surprised child. Then there's a rush and hubbub to get the youngster up, checked over, brushed off and the stanchions reset as everyone in the line watches.

Every season, some Santa Claus voyeurs visit every mall or Santa Claus special event in the region. Some will drive halfway across the state to see a special Santa Claus. The famous Richmond, Virginia, Miller & Rhoads department store Santa Claus, Bill Strother, drew folks from central and eastern North Carolina looking for "the real one."

Working both venues this season, I get to see many of the same visitors. Sometimes I am able to surprise them by remembering their names.

One little boy says, "Hey, look Mom, it's the same Santa we saw at the mall."

"Yes, Steve," I say, "Santa Claus gets around."

"He must be the real one," his Mother says, "He knows your name."

By 7:30 one night the visitor traffic in the tent is heavy, but moving smoothly. Piped-in holiday music, excited children, happy adults and Christmas Spirit fill the tent. From the chair, looking down the line I see a tall nerdy-looking dad and two children approach. The children, a girl and a boy, look to be seven and eight years old. The dad shows me his cameras and explains their unique features. They are designed to take two exposures simultaneously for a 3D picture.

His kids climb onto my lap. We all get set for the two-camera 3D shot: one youngster on each knee and my hand on each of their backs to stabilize them. Dad sights the cameras. Smiling, we lean forward for the shot. Then he calls out to his kids, "Pull his beard!" Each child grabs a fist full of my white whiskers and pulls. The camera flashes. "Oooooo!" I groan in pain. They're pulling off my face.

Letting go of the youngsters, I press my hands into my face and beard to stop the pain. I push the kids off my lap. They let go, land on their feet and walk away. I scold the dad, "Pulling on Santa Claus' beard hurts. It's not funny. It is painful and disrespectful."

The dad looks amused. Not saying a word, he turns and quickly walks away down the ramp. He has what he wanted: a picture of a surprised Santa Claus in pain. He leaves behind a fuming Santa Claus. I take in a couple of deep yoga breaths to calm myself. I have to stay in character and remember the next visitor is another opportunity to spread cheer and joy of the Christmas Spirit. I cannot imagine what motivated the "bad dad." I replay the scene and my response in my mind for days.

Then Santa Claus worked his magic.

Four days after the beard pulling incident, the dad and his two kids approach the Santa Claus Throne at Crabtree

Valley Mall. The dad tells the helper he will use his own camera. I recognize him and his cameras. Standing up from the throne, taking a deep breath, making myself as big as possible, I step into their path with my hands on my hips. Looking up, neither the dad nor the kids recognize me. Apparently all Santas look alike to them.

Giving the dad an intense and hard look, and with a grand gesture of pointing at him, I say, in a booming voice, "You are going to reap the pain of encouraging your children to misbehave. Telling them to pull Santa Claus's beard is mean and hateful."

Recognition flashes across his face. He immediately begins to apologize, saying, "I'm sorry, but I wanted an authentic 3D picture with a 'real' Santa Claus." I escort him and his children off the set. I wonder how many other Santa beards have been yanked or pulled off by this bad dad's kids. Beard pulling is a real challenge to the Santa Claus character.

For several years the Celebration of Lights was the most popular and most visited holiday venue in the Triangle. However, its popularity may have been a factor in its eventual closing. The two Interstate highway exits to the amphitheater nightly backed up with traffic extending into the travel lanes. Disagreement between The City and the lights' vendor happened when the city scheduled a concert that did not allow the vendor enough time to set up the elaborate display. Complaining that city workers were careless with his lights and gave out too many free passes, the vendor decided he couldn't set up his lights. In September 2006 the Convention and Visitors' Bureau staff recommended that the Raleigh City Council close the Celebration of Lights at Walnut Creek Amphitheater. The new Raleigh Convention Center was finished and ready to open. The staff had new priorities and turned off the lights. Now the city has very profitable holiday concert series there.

A couple of years before it closed, I had a memorable visitor.

She looks like a grandmother bundled against the cold, leaning on crutches; her right leg is in a white cast. She stands beside the visitors' line, watching it snake its way through the gold cord labyrinth. I look up, see her in the crowd of curious onlookers and hear my heart's small voice say, "She needs a Santa Claus hug." But she isn't in line; she isn't coming to see Santa. So, I stand up and follow a group of visitors as they exit down the ramp. Passing quickly through the crowd, I go to her and say, "Santa Claus wants to give you a hug."

Surprised, she looks up and says, "Okay." She slowly raises her arms, still holding her crutches with her armpits, and puts her arms around my big tummy and her face on my fur front. I wrap fur-cuffed arms around her shoulders, hold her snugly, and say quietly, "Santa Claus blesses you."

Our physical contact seems to generate a shared energy, a sense of relief and deep comfort. Our sharing complete, the hug ends. I pull back, holding her hands as I look into her moist eyes and say, "Merry Christmas, Happy New Year, and remember Santa Claus loves you." Turning, I scurry back up the exit ramp to the big green chair where the next family is waiting: three adults and four children. The kids sit on the arms of the chair, the adults gather around the back for their family photo. Two of the adults and two of the children are visiting their family in Cary for the holidays. They are from Cleveland, Ohio. I am surprised to learn the woman I have just hugged is their visiting Ohio grandmother.

The following holiday season the same family from Ohio and Cary came to visit with sad news: Grandmom had died a month earlier. They reported that on her deathbed she reminded her family Santa Claus had hugged her and told her he loved her. My heart swelled and tears came to my eyes. I remembered the energy and affection Grandmom and I had shared in our hug. I'm still mystified about what prompted me to go to her and ask for a hug. I had heard my heart's tiny voice say, "She needs a hug," and I acted on it. By listening, hearing and doing what my heart's small voice says, I can do good and share love.

A Parade

Every Santa Claus I know loves to be at the end of the Christmas Parade. Santa's arrival signals the beginning of the Holiday Season. He is a returning hero. Everyone is glad to see him, especially the children. He reminds us that good things are about to happen.

For twelve years on the first Saturday of December, beginning in 1999, SANTA AL worked the Durham Holiday Parade. During that time I witnessed the fading of the city's grand parade tradition. By 2010 the *Durham Herald-Sun* headline announced, "Yule parade deep-sixed in favor of festival – Diminished public participation factor in demise of 'Holiday Parade'." That was a great contrast to my first year. That year the Raleigh *News & Observer* reported an estimate of 40,000 folks in downtown Durham to watch or participate in the parade. Here I share some stories and tales about being at the end of the parade for over a decade.

Over the years the weather on the first weekend in December seemed to become more extreme. The time for the parade also shifted from mid-day to afternoon to evening. The freezing rain and ice cancelled the 2002 parade and closed down the region for two days.

My job at the end of the parade is to vigorously ring my sleigh bells, wave great big, loudly wish Merry Christmas and shout HO, HO, HOs! I try to make eye contact with everybody on both sides of the parade route, especially the children. My first year, there were dozens of sponsored parade floats, bands, marching units, decorated cars, trucks and service vehicles. The parade was televised live, taped and replayed on Christmas Day as part of the Triangle's Holiday celebration. Elizabeth Gardner of *WRAL News* hopped up on the float for a brief interview with Santa as the end of the parade passed the TV Camera reviewing stand. The crowd was so diverse that I could wish all, "Merry Christmas! Feliz Navidad! Happy Hanukkah! Joyous Kwanzaa! Happy New Year! Happy Holidays! with lots of HO, HO, HOs! Athletic Elizabeth leaped off the float with the microphone in her left hand, wishing Santa Claus "Happy Holidays!"

The next year Santa and Mrs. Claus were put on the top of a pumper fire truck. I was up so high I had to duck when the truck passed under traffic lights. The cold rain was steady. It rained and rained. Both of us were soaked through our fur. In addition to the parade, we were to make an appearance on stage in Durham's old baseball diamond two hours after the parade ended. Thank goodness for the Durham Fire Department. The fireman put us in the back of the fire truck cab and turned up the heat. We listened to the diesel engine purr. The chill was off our bodies when it was time for us to go back out in the rain and sing Christmas Carols at the ballpark.

After the September 11, 2001 attack, the entire country was frightened. Santa was put in the bucket of the hook and ladder fire truck. I was barely visible and had to stand on my tippy toes to see out and down to where folks lined the streets and sidewalks. As an additional security, a dozen Parks and Recreation staff members in bright yellow T-shirts walked in a phalanx semi-circle behind the fire truck. Three Durham County Sheriff cruisers followed them with two deputies in each. The deputy riding "shotgun" actually had one. It was a very warm 78 degrees.

I would be in the parade for 45 minutes to an hour, at the end of which my throat is horse, my arms are sore from waving and ringing the bells and eyes strained trying to look at each individual, The organizers do not allow anyone to throw or pass out candy to the crowds. It's a safety concern, not to have children out in the streets or in the parade trying pick up candy.

The parade route was always changing. A year later the parade ended in East Durham. After the parade I get a ride back to my van parked at the staging area, usually with a uniformed police officer. The crowd was disbursed and the officer and I were walking to his cruiser. As I was getting in the car the officer put his hand on the top of my Santa hat to help me get in. Just then a six-year-old boy and his grandmother were walking by and I heard him say, "Look Granny, they are taking Santa Claus downtown." He thought Santa Claus was under arrest.

Again the parade route changed. This time it started at the new *Durham Bulls* baseball stadium south of the railroad tracks, snaked its way north through downtown, crossing the tracks and ending at the old baseball park. As the parade turned behind City Hall Plaza, I felt something hit the seat of the float. My sleigh bells lost their rich ringing tone. The leather thong, which held all four bells to the leather strap, had torn. One bell hit the seat, another hit the street. As I sought to salvage what I could, leaving the bell on the seat and re-tying the remaining two, I looked down and back up the street to see the fourth bell bouncing toward the crowd on the sidewalk. A young boy let go of his mother's hand, ran out, and with one hand scooped up the bouncing bell. At first it seemed he wanted to bring it back to me, but the parade kept moving. I heard his mother say, "You have a bell from Santa's sleigh." They must have seen the new animated movie *The Polar Express,* where the greatest gift that year was a bell from Santa's sleigh. If you believe in Santa Claus, you will hear the sleigh bell ring.

The next year Bright Leaf Square shopping center sponsored the Santa float. I had a rocking chair for Santa visits both before and after the parade. I had about 300 visitors. The weather was beautiful: bright blue sky, a cool gentle breeze and warm sun.

The starting time for the parade was changed so that when the parade was over it would be dark enough to light Durham's first downtown Christmas Tree in the new CCB Plaza. From where the parade ended, I had six long blocks back up a steep hill to get to the Plaza for the tree lighting. The organizers hired an environmentally sound and visitor-friendly mode of transportation, a Greenway Transit pedi-cab. It's like a rickshaw on a bicycle frame with really low gearing. Although huffing and puffing, the operator soon delivered my 270 pounds up the hill to the Plaza. There I helped Wool E. Bull, the *Durham Bulls* baseball team mascot, and Durham Mayor Bill Bell to throw the switch that lit the tree. A burst of color from a tall and beautifully decorated North Carolina Douglas fir brought "ooohs" and "ahhaas" from the crowd.

I asked the mayor what he wanted for Christmas. He replied, "A peaceful holiday in Durham." As a rail trail advocate and a founder of Durham's American Tobacco Trail, I told the Mayor that Santa wanted the city to complete the 22-mile rail trail by building its bridge over Interstate Highway 40. He said, "I knew that."

The weather was terrible for the 2009 parade. As the parade started, there came a cold blustery wind-driven rain. As it got dark it got colder. The organizers had erected an open tent for the Santa Chair, but the wind was blowing the rain right into it. I missed the signal, if it were ever given, to come and help Wool E. Bull throw the switch to light the tree. The tree was less than half the size of the previous one. The Mayor, city council and most of the senior staff had gone to a "training conference."

Thank goodness for the strong and determined pedicab operator. He transported Wool E. Bull and me back across the railroad tracks, where Wool E. got out at the Bull's locker room. In the dark, cold rain and wind the operator peddled three more long blocks to my van. It was Durham's last Holiday Parade. The next year Durham had a Holiday Festival.

In all my years of doing Santa Claus, I have heard many requests for gifts, from a horse to a surfboard. One thing that folks always ask for is snow. We don't get much in the Piedmont of North Carolina, but in 2010 I was finally able to deliver.

The Santa chair sat onstage in the heated armory. I received my first visitor at 1:30 p.m. The photographer wanted to sell photos of visits with Santa, but by 2010 everyone had a digital camera or a cell phone camera. She didn't sell many photos. But, she told me, "You must be the 'real Santa,' you actually talk to the kids. The last Santa I worked with, the only thing he said was, 'Next!'"

About 2 p.m. I noticed through the windows that snow had begun to fall — big fat flakes. In a grand voice I called everyone's attention to the snow. "Look! It's snowing! Santa Claus has brought snow to Durham." Excitement filled the hall.

Later a young boy asked, "Santa, how did you bring the snow?"

"Oh, you want to know how Santa brought the snow?" I said. "Well, with a little Santa magic, and besides, I know the weatherman, Ho, Ho, Ho!"

Thick snow still fell an hour later as I climbed into the pedicab. The lightly clad lass operator wore a reindeer antlers headpiece. The canvas canopy and my water repellent cape protected me, but my driver worked in the falling snow. I hoped her peddling kept her warm. I could see only halfway down the block through the dense white blizzard. The five-block "mini parade" route circled the bank and the plaza. The Riverside High School Marching Band led the short parade of six units with Santa's pedicab bringing up the rear.

The snow hitting the pedicab peddler melted. She was snow-soaked and sweaty as she pressed on. Back in the armory the excitement had become worry, then dread, and finally panic. The Festival stopped. The tree lighting was cancelled. Everyone left hoping to get home safely.

I started Comet, my silver Toyota Sienna minivan, and scooped off more than three inches of snow from the windshield and hood. I felt confident in Comet's all wheel drive for the 28-mile trip home.

Snow still fell in Durham. The snow accumulation in nearby Chapel Hill was nil. The melting slush on the asphalt ended as I drove further south into Chatham County. I saw thin patches of snow here and there on the way, but none greeted me at home in Pittsboro.

From what I could see, downtown Durham and parts of north Raleigh had their own special snow dump. To me, this blizzard was a memorable gift from Santa Claus, a white snowy send-off from my last Durham Christmas event.

The next year the city hired a younger, cheaper and agile Santa Claus. It was a struggle for me to get in and out of the pedicab. Santa's parade rides had gone from a fancy reindeer sleigh float to a fire truck, to a pedicab.

I don't know how to explain the demise of the Durham's Holiday Parade. Raleigh Merchants' Christmas Parade is reported to be the biggest parade between Atlanta, GA and Washington, D.C. After 65 years Charlotte's Carolinas Carrousel Thanksgiving Day parade ended in 2012. Its corporate sponsor pulled out. Still the smaller cities in the Triangle like Knightdale, Wake Forest, Garner, Hillsborough and Pittsboro have their own local Holiday parades. Durham now has a Holiday Festival, not a parade. But Santa Claus is still there. Santa Claus has come to town. Merry Christmas and Ho, Ho, Ho!.

Hope Always

When Santa Claus shares the Christmas Spirit, Santa Claus shares hope. Hope informs our intent. Intent, combined with determination, imagination, and creativity, shapes our future. The habit of hope in SANTA AL spills over into my life as Al. In one difficult situation, I said to myself, "I believe I can help."

I live in North Carolina on the western edge of the Research Triangle and subscribe to two regional newspapers. The Raleigh *News & Observer* arrives between 3:30 and 4:00 a.m. The *Durham Herald-Sun* drops in the driveway between 8:30 and 9:30 a.m.

One morning about 8:40, seated at my computer reading my email, I heard steps on the front porch. I thought CR, my wife, had come back from her morning walk. The heavy rap on the glass storm door surprised me. Why would CR be knocking on her own front door?

I swiveled around in my chair to see — standing outside looking through the glass — a diminutive, stoop-shouldered, dark-skinned black woman with a pinched nose and thick horn-rimmed glasses. The door's brass edges framed her silhouette. With her hair pulled up on the back of her head, she looked like a black crested blue jay. It was Mary, the *Durham Herald-Sun* newspaper carrier.

I got up, opened the door as she put the newspaper, wrapped in a plastic sleeve, in my hand. She looked me in the eye and said, "Can you loan me ten dollars until tomorrow? I need to buy gas to get back to Chapel Hill."

I said, "Well, yeah. Wait, let me see if I've got it." I left her on the porch. I found my wallet. I had a couple of twenties, two fives and several ones. I thought a twenty would buy enough gas to get her Chrysler 300 back home. And, if she needs ten dollars, surely twenty would be better. I went back out and said, "This should be enough to get you back home." I handed her the $20 dollar bill and told her, "It's a gift."

Tears began to run down her cheeks. She told me her purse had been stolen the day before at the newspaper sub-station in Chapel Hill. She had lost her money, driver's license and important personal papers. The police had found nothing. Everything was gone. Trying to comfort her, I put my arm around her, telling her I was sorry for her loss. It was just bad luck.

It was then I thought, perhaps I have some power that could help in her recovery. I had shown sympathy, given her money, and still I could give her something else. I could give her some "Santa Claus Good Luck."

I said, "I believe I can help you change your luck." Back in the house, I got my SANTA AL business card. It's a laminated card with a picture of a waving, smiling Santa on one side, a logo and contact information on the other. I stepped down to the top step. She stood on the porch facing me. We were face to face.

I said, "Mary, let me tell you a story. One day in Charlotte I was buying gas. I went in to pay the clerk. As I did, she reached across the counter and pulled on my beard. 'Ouch!' I said, 'Why did you do that?"

She said, "My grandmother told me if I pulled on Santa's beard and it didn't come off I'd get Santa Claus Good Luck."

"As hard as you pulled you must need lots of good luck," I said.

I told Mary, "You can get Santa Claus Good Luck by touching Santa's beard."

I asked for her right hand. First she wanted to shake my hand. Her hand was large for her size and felt strong. I opened her hand and with a caressing motion guided it to rub the left side of my beard.

That morning I had used Cowboy Magic Conditioner on my beard. I learned about this horse-mane conditioner from Santa Tim's School4Santa in Greensboro in 2009. It feels like silicone, gives a sheen and more body to the beard, and leaves a pleasant, distinctive fragrance. Letting go of my beard, she put her head on my shoulder and began to sob. I embraced her, telling her, "It will be all right. You will be just fine. You've got some Santa Claus Good

Luck now."

She slowly quieted and began to breathe deeply. I gave her my Santa card, saying, "What you need now is a smile." When I give a Santa card, I tell folks I'm giving them a smile. "Any time you need a smile, all you have to do is look at this card. You see a waving Santa with a big smile. When you see a smile, what do you do? You smile." The top of the card reads "Merry Christmas," the bottom, "Love, SANTA AL."

She insisted she wanted to pay me back. But I said, "No, No! This is a gift from Santa Claus. What Santa wants you to do is to keep coming back to bring him his Durham newspaper." She took the card and hugged me again, saying, "God Bless You." I gave a soft little "Ho, Ho, Ho" chuckle. Then she was down the steps and off.

Back at the computer, I realized and appreciated the magical power of hope available to us all when we show love, care and concern for one another. It is like Christmas.

Three days later the *Herald-Sun* did not arrive until 1:30 p.m. Early that morning a large deer had run into the front of her Chrysler, damaging its radiator. Mary had to borrow a friend's car to finish delivering her route. I thought, at least the deer did not crash into her windshield. Maybe that was her Santa Claus Good Luck.

By the end of the month we had a new and more timely carrier. Concerned about Mary, CR sent her a $25 Food Lion gift card. She got a nice thank you note in return. Mary really needed the help. Then we read in the Chatham newspaper that Mary had been charged with shoplifting.

The charges were dropped when she made restitution. Had her luck changed? It did not seem so, but her circumstances had changed and hopefully in that change she found the opportunities she needed to improve her life.

Being real-bearded, I look like Santa Claus all year round. But it is in the fall when folks start thinking about Christmas and seeing images of Santa Claus in me. I love to visit the North Carolina State Fair each year in October with my wife. One year at the NCSU Ice Cream stand I waited for her while she stood in line for our Pecan-Heath Bar milk shake. Dressed in ordinary clothes, I leaned on my walking sticks. A young mother pushing a green, doublewide stroller had two little girls hanging on her coat. She stopped in front of me and set the brakes. I don't think the mother had expected to see Santa Claus at the State Fair, but when she saw me, I heard her say to her kids, "I think I see Santa Claus."

The two little girls left her side and walked up to me. The five-year-old held her 3½-year-old sister's hand. Pointing at her sister, she said, "She has a question for you."

"Yes," I said. As I leaned over I reached into my left front pocket for a couple of Santa cards. Looking up at me, the little sister asked, "Are you Santa Claus?"

After a slight pause, I repeated her question, "Am I Santa Claus? Well, I have a question for you." Turning my head slightly, I asked, "Have you been being good?"

The little sister looked straight at me said, "Yes, I've

been good."

"And has your big sister been good?"

"Oh, yes sir, she's been good, too," she replied.

"Great," I said, "Then Santa Claus has something for you." I gave each girl a Santa card.

Then I asked, "Whose picture is on your card?

They looked at their cards and together said, "It's Santa Claus, it's you!" They shrieked, jumping up and down, holding on to one another. "It's him! It's him! It's Santa Claus!"

I put my right index finger up to my lips, smiled big, and with an exaggerated wink I said, "Let's keep this our secret."

Beaming, the mom held the long push bar of the doublewide. I noticed the blanket covering the far seat move. The blanket fell off the head and shoulders of their red-haired two-year-old little brother. He took his thumb out of his mouth and reached up for a Santa card. As he did, I reached over, gave him his card and reminded him to be good, too. Not wanting to be seen by Santa Claus, he'd apparently covered himself when he heard his mom say, "I think I see Santa Claus."

CR and I sat on a Farm Bureau bench in front of the Hobbies and Crafts Building, and shared our milkshake. We saw the family leave, each child holding their own Santa card. The 3½-year-old turned back for one last look. I waved a little secret wave. She smiled, waved back, and disappeared into the crowd with her family. Perhaps she was thinking of what her mother had said, "You are likely to see

Santa Claus anywhere, at any time, so you better be good."

Being a naturally bearded Santa Claus, my sensitivities are heightened when folks look at me. I need to determine who they are seeing: an old man or Santa in street clothes. It might be a quick second look, it might be a smile, it might be a concentrated effort not to look, or simply a stare.

Just after Thanksgiving, in the grocery store I saw a young girl about nine years old do a double take. Her folks stood with an empty cart at the end of the aisle. She was plain. Her clothes looked worn and little faded, but clean.

Her actions alerted me to the likelihood she saw me as Santa. I paused, looked her in the eye, and said, "What do you want for Christmas?" Looking back at me, she said, "We can't afford to have Santa Claus stop at our house."

Taken back, I felt sad for her and a little embarrassed for having asked the question. Her Santa's visit had a price tag. In the third verse of Gene Autry's song *Here Comes Santa Claus,* he sings,

> *He doesn't care if you're rich or poor*
> *He loves you just the same*
> *Santa Claus knows we're all God's children*
> *That makes everything right,*
> *So fill your hearts with Christmas cheer*
> *'Cause Santa Claus comes tonight!*

I took out a small, individually wrapped candy cane from my jacket pocket, gave it to her, and said, "Merry Christmas."

Her parents watched from the end of the aisle. Her mother called out, "Ann, come along now." Ann looked at her candy cane, then me, turned quickly and walked briskly toward her mom. Had she seen Santa Claus? Together they turned and rounded the corner. I didn't see them after that. On second thought, I wish I'd given her the candy cane without the question.

Santa's presence is a blessing. Hope continues to be his message. For children and adults in circus tents, malls, at parades and even at the State Fair on an ordinary day, the Christmas Spirit is a presence and a blessing available to all of us. So,

"Happy Christmas to all and to all a good night."

Christmas Future

In my world, Santa Claus is an independent self-employed businessman. For Santa, Mrs. Claus, and related elves, the IRS occupational code is 541990: Entertainer. As in any business, there are occupational hazards. I experience aching thighs from heavy visitors, blurry vision from the repeated bright camera flashes, frayed nerves from dealing with screaming toddlers, insensitive Santa set managers and belligerent adults. Sixteen years of mall Santa work have taken a toll on my body. But it is all worth it for the heartfelt smiles and shared Christmas cheer I see and feel as the results of my SANTA AL work.

Still, there are things about the working life of Santa that have troubled me from the moment of that first photo shoot on the carousel, where the mall decided they did not need to pay to use my image. Sometimes Santas are not paid for their work. All the Santas I know do charity work. But Santa Claus work is a business that has to sustain itself, as well as the man behind the Santa smile, if it is to continue. I've had clients say, "We should not have to pay you, Santa, because you have too much fun." As you have seen, Santa work may be deeply satisfying and fun, but it also requires professional skills, expensive equipment, travel and commitment. Santas deserve to be paid.

Over the years I have seen structural problems in the Santa services in our area. The season is short and most of the work is on weekends. Sometimes there is too much work and not enough Santas. Sometimes people hire Santa workers who haven't much training, if any. And the quality of the Santa service is not up to par.

By 2003 I was getting more requests for appearances than I could fulfill. I was working the mall during weekdays, the Celebration of Lights at night, and private parties, parades and country clubs on the weekends. I was overwhelmed. I needed help. That's when Santa Claus gave me an idea: I could get support for my work, and help others, too, if I organized a network of Santa Buddies.

Santa Buddies, I envisioned, would be a group of working Santas who could support one another by sharing advice, discussing experiences, seeking training and making referrals for work with each other. By banding together we could be more assured in our work negotiations. We could encourage each other to do our best and to further our training and knowledge. Mall and event managers could benefit, too, by having a one-stop source of reliable and experienced Santas.

I already had five Santa colleagues.

Santa Dwight Compton (Cedar Grove) was a mall Santa at South Square when I was first hired there in 1992. We did tag team Santa work for years.

Santa Bryce Bates (Durham) worked at Northgate Mall.

Santa George McKellar (Raleigh) and Santa Steve Gattis (Raleigh) I recruited when I saw them walking through Crabtree Mall. They both began their Santa careers working fill-in at the Celebration of Lights. SANTA DWIGHT recruited his friend, Santa Charlie Easton (Oxford).

Our first meeting was the third Wednesday, April 20th 2005. We met at the Ole NC BBQ in north Durham. We all ate from the buffet and ate well. We met in their small meeting room. Several of the Santas brought their curious wives. For the program we examined the quality of the super professional Santa suit from Santa & Co. and watched a portion of an A&E Biography video about Santa Claus.

Every professional Santa has his own suit or suits. SANTA CHARLIE's wife volunteered to make his suit. For his appearance in the Oxford Parade he had used the city's suit. After our meeting my webmaster son, AC, added a Buddies page to SANTAAL.COM. It had pictures and contact information listed for each Buddy with the encouragement, "If you can't book SANTA AL, book one of his Buddies." Soon Buddies were recruiting other Santas or Santa want-to-bes.

The Buddies now meet six times throughout the year, for fellowship, to improve our Santa Claus knowledge and practice, and to support one another. We share stories, experiences, resources, do role plays of home visits, discuss relevant topics like how to be Santa Claus in a Muslim family photo and how to say appropriate phrases in Spanish. We host programs on self-employment taxes, business practices, the history of St. Nicholas and Santa Claus, how to improve our Santa Claus service network and upgrading our "Holiday Spirit." Above all, we help one another in fulfilling our commitment to quality Santa Claus services in the Research Triangle of North Carolina.

Typical Santa Claus wisdom encourages Santa to have another Santa as a friend and mentor. Over the years, I first learned about makeup from SANTA DWIGHT. For example, use a lifting motion when applying mascara to the eyebrows to create an elfin look. Later he let his beard grow and became a real-bearded Santa. He said it made him a better Santa because now he could focus on his visitor without worrying about his beard being pulled off. Now he looks like Santa all year round. Santa Steve Gillham's presentations on web links, story telling, audio equipment and schedule management informed me and helped all the Buddies.

SANTA BRYCE has been a mentor in my move toward doing hospice volunteering as Santa. He is a member of Santa America, a nationwide organization of hospice-trained Santas. He was trained by the Duke Medical Center. I was trained by UNC Hospice. He and I inducted my white-bearded 93-year-old patient Ben into the Triangle Santa Buddies in April 2013. That means a Santa Buddy will be at SANTA BEN's funeral. By being so helped, I'm able to help others. Only Santa Claus can really know and understand another Santa Claus. Our distinctive mission of spreading joy and sharing hope calls Santas into a special brotherhood.

At the beginning of the 2010 season, I got help to create a new website: www.TriangleSantaBuddies.com. Santa Al's Buddies had multiplied. Now there are 34 Santas on the roster. Some members were concerned there would not be enough work for so many Santas. However, that fear has not been realized. The spirit of Santa Claus has been at work: by sharing ourselves, we've discovered more opportunities for Santa Claus work.

When I first began recommending a Buddy to a client, I would feel I was losing a job. A different Santa getting paid for doing one of my gigs, I thought. Then I remembered the referral got a buddy a gig and opened time on my calendar for other opportunities to promote and extend the Spirit of Christmas.

These days, what started as Santa Al's Buddies has become its own independent organization: Triangle Santa Buddies, known to its members as the TSB. I continue to facilitate meetings with the help of my wife, CR Townsend (Elf Renee). We continue to grow. Some of us are in better physical shape than others. Santa's work is physical work. The TSB gather for fellowship and training led by fellow Santas rather than by the photo companies or malls. The TSB motto is, *"The more Santas there are, the more Christmas Spirit there is, but only one Santa in the mall at a time."*

Some large department stores and photo studio chains will bring their "own" Santa into the mall for special photo shoots. The mall management generally discourages this practice. The Santa is often slipped into the store by a back way. A second Santa creates a problem for the mall Santa, when the youngster says, "Santa, didn't I just see you in Belk's?" The mall Santa may reply, "Oh, you saw one of my Santa helpers, you continue to be good, now! Ho, Ho, Ho! Merry Christmas!"

What's worse is to have two mall Santas on the floor at the same time. I remember when SANTA DWIGHT and I were tag team Santas at Crabtree Mall in Raleigh. Switching the Santas could be tricky. Breaking the line and changing Santas required precision timing. It depended on clear and timely communications between the helpers escorting the second shift Santa. One time the first shift helpers kept me busy up to the last minute. The second shift helpers failed to alert the first shift of their departure from the Santa dressing room in the back hall on the second floor. As they looked down on the Santa set chair it was empty. I had just gotten up on my way to the elevator. The plan was for me to exit the mall through the second floor food court service door to the parking deck.

When the elevator doors opened on the second floor, there stood SANTA DWIGHT, the second shift Santa, waiting to get on. A cardinal rule in mall Santa Claus work is only one Santa in a mall at a time. There we stood facing each other: two 270-pound big-tummied white-bearded old men in identical Santa suits. Food court folks stopped and looked. Like on cue, we both reached out shook one another's gloved hand and with left hands on each other's shoulders slowly turned to the right and exchanged places while wishing each other, "Merry Christmas, Santa." It was as if we were tag team wrestlers, one coming out of the ring, the other going in. The elevator door closed. In a flash we went our separate ways, but the folks in the food court had seen a phenomenon, two Santas together in the mall at the same time. It was embarrassing for the both of us. Now we laugh about it, but we don't want it to happen again.

Santa's work is a business, says Santa Timothy Connaghan, RBS (Real Bearded Santa), also known as "Santa Hollywood," principal in the Kringle Group, LLC and Chancellor of his International University of Santa Claus. SANTA TIM conducts his two-day School4Santa workshops nationwide in major markets. In 2009 I took his course in Greensboro and earned a Santa Claus Bachelor's degree in SantaClausology. In 2012 I earned my Master's degree at his school in Lancaster, PA, the home of the National Christmas Museum. He also offers an Associate diploma through his DVD correspondence course, and a Ph.D. for helping him teach one of his workshops. SANTA TIM teaches from his textbook, *Behind the Red Suit – The Business of Santa Claus.* He discusses Santa's background, basics, directions, procedures and guidelines about the business of Santa Claus.

If "Santa Hollywood" teaches the business of Santa, the Charles W. Howard Santa Claus School teaches the heart. Begun in Albion, NY in 1937, Howard's aim was to perfect the role of Santa Claus. His students were from major department stores. He helped to convene the first Santa Claus Convention in 1939, in New York City. Portions of his curriculum are still used today by SANTA TOM and Mrs. Holly Valent in their C.W. Howard Santa Claus School in Midland, MI. The three-day school is conducted once a year in October with limited class size to about 60 students. The focus is upon the very special character of Santa Claus and his unique personal relationship with each of his visitors. Several Santas from TSB are graduates of this granddaddy Santa Claus School.

Christmas future will always include Santa Claus. Santa's job is to spread Christmas cheer. Just as the Spirit of Santa called the man behind the Santa smile that day on the mall's carousel to become SANTA AL, I believe Santa's Spirit calls us all to share in the joy and mystery of Christmas.

I believe Santa's Spirit also called me to help and nurture other Santas. Yes, Virginia, there is a Santa Claus, and he will exist forever in the hearts and minds of working Santas everywhere.

Afterword

When I began doing Santa Claus work, I also started to keep a daily journal of the experience. First, I wanted to accurately record my time going on and coming off the Santa Set to avoid any conflicts with management. Secondly, the journal helped me to draw a line under that day's experience, thus helping me to not carry the feelings of that day into the next. It also offered an opportunity to reflect upon the experience as a way of learning by doing.

Over the years of recording and collecting stories of the Santa work it occurred to me that I had experiences that might interest others. I had stories about the magic of Christmas and Santa Claus at work. At first I thought I'd write a memoir, but it bogged down with too much stuff. I engaged Marjorie Hudson, attended her Kitchen Table Writers' class, and enrolled in the Creative Writing Certificate Program at Central Carolina Community College, Pittsboro Campus. Three years later, in 2013, I was in the first graduating class of the writing program.

The dilemma for me was how to write about my Santa Claus work and not call myself Santa Claus. My first draft was in the third person, talking about Santa. For example, "Santa greeted his young visitor with a smile." But Melissa Delbridge and my colleagues at the college persuaded me a memoir is best told in the first person, so I rewrote it using the voice of SANTA AL as Santa Claus. Some remnants of the third person may remain, but I want it to be clear when SANTA AL is talking and when Santa Claus is talking. I feel as if I have become a ghostwriter for SANTA AL. And so, I think of the author as SANTA AL.

The twenty years of SANTA AL's Santa Claus work is located primarily in the Research Triangle region of North Carolina – anchored by the cities of Raleigh, Durham and Chapel Hill. The time frame is from 1992 to 2012. Some names have been changed.

My hope for you is that you find in these pages loving, poignant, humorous, and touching tales of the Santa Claus work and that you will be inspired to continue to believe in Santa Claus and the Spirit of Christmas.

Merry Christmas!
Love, SANTA AL
(AKA Al Capehart)

ABOUT THE AUTHOR

Born and reared in Richmond, Virginia, Al Capehart moved to North Carolina in 1957 to continue his education: B.A. in History, Pfeiffer University in Misenheimer; M.Div., Duke University in Durham; M.Ed., The University of NC at Chapel Hill; and a Ph.D. in Psychology, NC State University in Raleigh. When his Uncle Charlie heard Al had earned his Ph.D., he said, "I'm glad he has finally learned enough to get out of school."

Al was a founder and served as volunteer president of NC Rail-Trails for 20 years, received a Lifetime Achievement Award from the NC Land Trust Council in 2010 and was selected "Tarheel of the Week" by the Raleigh *News & Observer.* During the war on poverty in the 1960s and 70s, he taught night school, worked with school dropouts and directed the successful New Careers job training program.

By 2010, TRIANGLESANTABUDDIES.COM, the web site he had created in conjunction with the professional Santa association, featured 34 Santas on call. His poem *Happy Winter Home* won first place in the 2012 Chatham County Senior games Literary Arts competition. In 2013 he finished Central Carolina Community College's Certificate Program in Creative Writing in Pittsboro. He facilitates the "First Thursday Writing Family" support group, is a member of the NC Writers' Network, attends St. Bartholomew's Episcopal Church, and practices yoga.

With his wife Carolyn Renee (CR) and their cat Sandy Paws, he resides in Pittsboro, NC, among an assortment of Apple computers and motorized vehicles, all with endearing names. LT (Last Truck), Comet (his Santa dressing room minivan), and white-tailed deer families live in the yard, a leather strap of sleigh bells hangs on the front door, and a white stick Christmas tree with colored lights decorates the front porch near his rocking chair.

Behind Santa's Smile

92262876R00055

Made in the USA
San Bernardino, CA
07 November 2018